Waiting, Waiting, Waiting!

The Story of Simeon and Anna

We are grateful to the following team of authors for their contributions to *God Loves Me*, a Bible story program for young children. This Bible story, one of a series of fifty-two, was written by Patricia L. Nederveld, managing editor for CRC Publications. Suggestions for using this book were developed by Jesslyn DeBoer, a freelance author from Grand Rapids, Michigan. Yvonne Van Ee, an early childhood educator, served as project consultant and wrote *God Loves Me*, the program guide that accompanies this series of Bible storybooks.

Nederveld has served as a consultant to Title I early childhood programs in Colorado. She has extensive experience as a writer, teacher, and consultant for federally funded preschool, kindergarten, and early childhood programs in Colorado, Texas, Michigan, Florida, Missouri, and Washington, using the *High/Scope* Education Research Foundation curriculum. In addition to writing the *Bible Footprints* church curriculum for four- and five-year-old, Nederveld edited the revised *Threes* curriculum and the first edition of preschool through second grade materials for the *LiFE* curriculum, all published by CRC Publications.

DeBoer has served as a church preschool leader and as coauthor of the preschool-kindergarten materials for the *LiFE* curriculum published by CRC Publications. She has also written K-6 science and health curriculum for Christian Schools International, Grand Rapids, Michigan, and inspirational gift books for Zondervan Publishing House.

Van Ee is a professor and early childhood program advisor in the Education Department at Calvin College, Grand Rapids, Michigan. She has served as curriculum author and consultant for Christian Schools International and wrote the original *Story Hour* organization manual and curriculum materials for fours and fives.

Photo on page 5: Sue Ann Miller/Tony Stone Images; photo on page 20: SuperStock.

Library of Congress Cataloging-in-Publication Data

Nederveld, Patricia L., 1944-
   Waiting, waiting, waiting!: the story of Simeon and Anna/Patricia L. Nederveld.
      p. cm. — (God loves me; bk. 27)
   Summary: A simple retelling of the Bible story about how happy Simeon and Anna were when they saw the baby Jesus at the temple. Includes follow-up activities.
   ISBN 1-56212-296-7
   1. Jesus Christ—Presentation—Juvenile literature. [1. Jesus Christ—Presentation. 2. Bible stories—N.T.] I. Title.
   II. Series: Nederveld, Patricia L., 1944-   God loves me; bk. 27.
   BT319.N435   1998
   232.92'6—dc21   97-53309
                                                                                           CIP
                                                                                           AC

10 9 8 7 6 5 4 3 2 1

Waiting, Waiting, Waiting!

The Story of Simeon and Anna

PATRICIA L. NEDERVELD

ILLUSTRATIONS BY CATHY ANN JOHNSON

CRC Publications
Grand Rapids, Michigan

This is a story from God's book, the Bible.

It's for say name(s) of your child(ren).
It's for me too!

Luke 2:21-38

Waiting . . .
waiting . . .
waiting!
Simeon was
growing old. But
still he waited for
God to send baby
Jesus. God told
Simeon it would
happen soon!

And while Simeon
waited, he prayed.

Waiting . . . waiting . . . waiting! Anna was growing old. But still she waited for God to send baby Jesus. She hoped it would be soon!

And while Anna waited, she prayed.

Simeon waited. Simeon prayed. And Simeon watched! He watched everyone who came to the temple to worship God. Would he see baby Jesus soon? Each day he wondered . . .

A nna did too. She waited. She prayed. And she watched. Each day she wondered if this was the day she would see God's Son.

12

Then it happened. Mary and Joseph brought their precious little baby to God's temple.

Look, Simeon! Jesus is here! Look, Anna! Your waiting is over!

Happy Simeon held baby Jesus in his arms. He praised God. "You've kept your promise, Lord. Jesus, your Son, is here at last!"

Then it was Anna's turn. "Dear God, everyone has been waiting for you to send Jesus! Now he's here, and our waiting is over! Thank you, Lord!"

I wonder if it's hard for you to wait for happy things . . .

Dear God, thank you for sending baby Jesus. We're glad you love us so much! Amen.

Suggestions for Follow-up

Opening

As you spend time with your little ones today, talk about waiting—waiting for a turn to talk or to play with a favorite toy, waiting for help, waiting for someone to listen, waiting for Christmas, and so on. Acknowledge that it can be very hard to wait.

Before reading the story, tell the children you have a special treat for them. Bring individually wrapped snacks such as raisins or crackers or a small reward like stickers or pencils, and place them in a pretty bag. Tell the children that they must wait for the treat and listen quietly to the story first. After children respond to the "I wonder" statement on page 21, give each child a treat. Praise your little ones for waiting so patiently!

Learning Through Play

Learning through play is the best way! The following activity suggestions are meant to help you provide props and experiences that will invite the children to play their way into the Scripture story and its simple truth. Try to provide plenty of time for the children to choose their own activities and to play individually. Use group activities sparingly—little ones learn most comfortably with a minimum of structure.

1. As children enjoy dramatic play, look for ways to incorporate everyday examples of waiting and getting ready for good things to happen. Encourage children to pretend they are waiting for a birthday party or waiting for a grandparent to come for a visit. Suggest that children prepare special food, clean the house, check out the window.

2. Make a photocopy of the prayer on page 21. Enlarge to about twice the size and make one copy per child. Then cut out the framed prayers and glue them to an 8" (20 cm) square of posterboard, leaving a border all around. Invite children to decorate the borders of the prayer posters. Set out large star stickers, bits of lace and ribbon, trim from old Christmas cards, and the like. Pour small amounts of glue into shallow containers so children can dip the trims in the glue. Read the prayer several times to the children as they work.

3. You can use the song "He Came Down" (Songs Section, *God Loves Me* program guide) for worship and praise. Invite an older child to play the song on a recorder, or play the piano as you sing the song for your little ones. Offer them crepe-paper streamers to wave to the rhythm. Encourage your children to join in on the words of the song printed in bold below:

   > He came down that we may have **love**;
   > he came down that we may have **love**;
   > he came down that we may have **love**.
   > **Hallelujah** for evermore.
   > —Traditional

4. Make up a waiting game. Take one or two children by the hand, and invite them to follow your lead. Take a few giant steps and then say, "Let's rest and wait while I count to five." Then stretch one arm out to reach

another child to join you. Say, "Let's all hold hands and wait right here while I count to five." Keep on adding children and new activities (touching toes, sitting in a circle, walking fast, and so forth). Pause each time to count to five—or ten if your children can really wait longer. Praise your children for waiting—even when they're excited and full of energy!

Closing

Gather your little ones around you and talk about the different ways the children practiced waiting today. Remind them of Simeon's and Anna's long, long wait for baby Jesus. Name each child as you tell your little ones how happy you are God sent Jesus for them. Use the prayer on page 21 to wrap up your time together.

At Home

It's often very hard for little ones to wait patiently. Make up silly tunes about waiting patiently, count backwards to measure "take-off" time, set a timer or an alarm clock to signal your child's routines, read a book about impatient animals or slow, pokey ones. Celebrate special moments together each day, and remind your little one how happy you are that God gave you *two* gifts—Jesus and your little one!

Old Testament Stories

Blue and Green and Purple Too! *The Story of God's Colorful World*

It's a Noisy Place! *The Story of the First Creatures*

Adam and Eve *The Story of the First Man and Woman*

Take Good Care of My World! *The Story of Adam and Eve in the Garden*

A Very Sad Day *The Story of Adam and Eve's Disobedience*

A Rainy, Rainy Day *The Story of Noah*

Count the Stars! *The Story of God's Promise to Abraham and Sarah*

A Girl Named Rebekah *The Story of God's Answer to Abraham*

Two Coats for Joseph *The Story of Young Joseph*

Plenty to Eat *The Story of Joseph and His Brothers*

Safe in a Basket *The Story of Baby Moses*

I'll Do It! *The Story of Moses and the Burning Bush*

Safe at Last! *The Story of Moses and the Red Sea*

What Is It? *The Story of Manna in the Desert*

A Tall Wall *The Story of Jericho*

A Baby for Hannah *The Story of an Answered Prayer*

Samuel! Samuel! *The Story of God's Call to Samuel*

Lions and Bears! *The Story of David the Shepherd Boy*

David and the Giant *The Story of David and Goliath*

A Little Jar of Oil *The Story of Elisha and the Widow*

One, Two, Three, Four, Five, Six, Seven! *The Story of Elisha and Naaman*

A Big Fish Story *The Story of Jonah*

Lions, Lions! *The Story of Daniel*

New Testament Stories

Jesus Is Born! *The Story of Christmas*

Good News! *The Story of the Shepherds*

An Amazing Star! *The Story of the Wise Men*

Waiting, Waiting, Waiting! *The Story of Simeon and Anna*

Who Is This Child? *The Story of Jesus in the Temple*

Follow Me! *The Story of Jesus and His Twelve Helpers*

The Greatest Gift *The Story of Jesus and the Woman at the Well*

A Father's Wish *The Story of Jesus and a Little Boy*

Just Believe! *The Story of Jesus and a Little Girl*

Get Up and Walk! *The Story of Jesus and a Man Who Couldn't Walk*

A Little Lunch *The Story of Jesus and a Hungry Crowd*

A Scary Storm *The Story of Jesus and a Stormy Sea*

Thank You, Jesus! *The Story of Jesus and One Thankful Man*

A Wonderful Sight! *The Story of Jesus and a Man Who Couldn't See*

A Better Thing to Do *The Story of Jesus and Mary and Martha*

A Lost Lamb *The Story of the Good Shepherd*

Come to Me! *The Story of Jesus and the Children*

Have a Great Day! *The Story of Jesus and Zacchaeus*

I Love You, Jesus! *The Story of Mary's Gift to Jesus*

Hosanna! *The Story of Palm Sunday*

The Best Day Ever! *The Story of Easter*

Goodbye—for Now *The Story of Jesus' Return to Heaven*

A Prayer for Peter *The Story of Peter in Prison*

Sad Day, Happy Day! *The Story of Peter and Dorcas*

A New Friend *The Story of Paul's Conversion*

Over the Wall *The Story of Paul's Escape in a Basket*

A Song in the Night *The Story of Paul and Silas in Prison*

A Ride in the Night *The Story of Paul's Escape on Horseback*

The Shipwreck *The Story of Paul's Rescue at Sea*

Holiday Stories

Selected stories from the New Testament to help you celebrate the Christian year

Jesus Is Born! *The Story of Christmas*

Good News! *The Story of the Shepherds*

An Amazing Star! *The Story of the Wise Men*

Hosanna! *The Story of Palm Sunday*

The Best Day Ever! *The Story of Easter*

Goodbye—for Now *The Story of Jesus' Return to Heaven*

These fifty-two books are the heart of *God Loves Me,* a Bible story program designed for young children. Individual books (or the entire set) and the accompanying program guide *God Loves Me* are available from CRC Publications (1-800-333-8300).